50 TH
BOOK SERIES
REVIEWS FROM READERS

I recently downloaded a couple of books from this series to read over the weekend thinking I would read just one or two. However, I so loved the books that I read all the six books I had downloaded in one go and ended up downloading a few more today. Written by different authors, the books offer practical advice on how you can perform or achieve certain goals in life, which in this case is how to have a better life.

The information is simple to digest and learn from, and is incredibly useful. There are also resources listed at the end of the book that you can use to get more information.

50 Things To Know To Have A Better Life: Self-Improvement Made Easy! by Dannii Cohen

---

This book is very helpful and provides simple tips on how to improve your everyday life. I found it to be useful in improving my overall attitude.

50 Things to Know For Your Mindfulness & Meditation Journey by Nina Edmondso

---

Quick read with 50 short and easy tips for what to think about before starting to homeschool.

50 Things to Know About Getting Started with Homeschool by Amanda Walton

I really enjoyed the voice of the narrator, she speaks in a soothing tone. The book is a really great reminder of things we might have known we could do during stressful times, but forgot over the years.

- HarmonyHawaii

50 Things to Know to Manage Your Stress: Relieve The Pressure and Return The Joy To Your Life

by Diane Whitbeck

There is so much waste in our society today. Everyone should be forced to read this book. I know I am passing it on to my family.

50 Things to Know to Downsize Your Life: How To Downsize, Organize, And Get Back to Basics

by Lisa Rusczyk Ed. D.

Great book to get you motivated and understand why you may be losing motivation. Great for that person who wants to start getting healthy, or just for you when you need motivation while having an established workout routine.

50 Things To Know To Stick With A Workout: Motivational Tips To Start The New You Today

by Sarah Hughes

50 THINGS TO KNOW ABOUT LEARNING A FOREIGN LANGUAGE

Expand your Language Skills

Megan Orthmann

CZYK Publishing Since 2011.

50 Things to Know
Visit our website at www.50thingstoknow..com

Lock Haven, PA
All rights reserved.
ISBN: 9781793137111

50 THINGS TO KNOW ABOUT LEARNING A FOREIGN LANGUAGE

BOOK DESCRIPTION

This book is a summary of everything needed to begin learning a foreign language, including the first steps to take, available resources, and how new languages can change your life. Within these pages there are practical methods and personal experiences to help guide you in language learning journey. In addition to finding various learning tools, there are anecdotes about how languages can affect your mind and perspective on the world.

1) How do you begin learning a foreign language?
2) What are resources that language learners use?
3) What can you gain from learning a new language?

If you answered yes to any of these questions then this book is for you...

50 Things to Know About Learning A Foreign Language by Megan Orthmann offers an approach to learning any foreign language with tips and tricks to succeed. Most books on language learning tell you to take formal classes, study verb charts, and spend years memorizing verb lists. Although there's nothing

wrong with those approaches, there is never a single way to learn a new skill. Learning a language is much easier and more relaxed than it appears. Many people believe that in order to learn any language you must be just, "good at learning languages." So many people believe they are not someone with this natural ability. Everyone, no matter your strengths, weaknesses, age, or financial situation, can learn a language.

In these pages you'll discover language learning methods, helpful advice, and everything you need to know about the learning process. This book will help you to begin your journey by picking a language you will enjoy, teach you how to gain confidence and skills, and use the language to your best ability with native and experienced speakers. There is more to language learning than memorizing words and verbs, see for yourself how much perspective learning a new language can give you.

By the time you finish this book, you will know how to begin learning any languages and the mental and physical tools to do it! So, grab YOUR copy today. You'll be glad you did.

TABLE OF CONTENTS

Other Helpful Resources:
50 Things to Know

DEDICATION

To all my past language teachers that have given me inspiration, support, and guidance.

ABOUT THE AUTHOR

Megan Orthmann is a lifetime language learner and traveler. She is a native English speaker from the United States. Megan began studying languages at the age of 12, when she discovered an electronic translator for Spanish, French, and German. Since that time, she has studied various languages in order to travel the world. She was also an International Studies and French Language major in college. Throughout her lifetime (so far), Megan has studied languages such as Spanish, French, German, Italian, American Sign Language, Brazilian Portuguese, and even a bit of Korean and Mandarin Chinese. Megan's goals are to speak at least 5 languages in order to meet new, interesting people from around the globe. She currently lives in Minnesota, USA, part-time. The rest of the time, she is traveling and teaching English as a Second Language in various countries around the world.

INTRODUCTION

*"The limits of my language
mean the limits of my world."*

– Ludwig Wittgenstein

Learning a language can seem daunting at first. All you can focus on is millions of new words and sounds you don't recognize. So, how do you start? It's entirely possible and not nearly as scary as it sounds.

I firmly believe that anyone can learn a new language, if you invest enough time and effort. Start small and build your skills day-by-day. There is no magic method to fluency in "one month" or less, so be wary about the idea that language learning is instantaneous and the same for everyone. Learning a foreign language takes time, but it doesn't have to take forever! You'll be amazed when months pass by and your ability continues to grow. Soon six months later you'll find yourself having conversations with native speakers. You don't remember the exact moment a change took place, but somehow all that work has paid off.

Below are 50 things you should know about learning a language. Included are some tips on how to begin learning a language from the absolute basics to a more advanced ability. This includes how to get a good feel for the language and understand its sound, pattern, and voice. From there, you'll find ways to advance through the language learning difficulties and levels until you find yourself using your target language daily! Lastly, there will be plenty of advice on little pieces of information you may not have known about learning a language and how it may affect you. For example: did you know that one day you may dream or think in another language? Keep reading to discover more…

1. PICKING A LANGUAGE

If you're reading this, you've probably picked a language to learn or you're still in the process of deciding. Whatever the case, this is the first step in learning any language. Asses the reason that you want to learn a specific language. Do you need it for work? Or, are you trying to strike up a conversation with a new friend? Whatever your reason for choosing, it's crucial to adjust your expectations. If you're learning a language that is closely related to your native language, it may be slightly easier to do. For example, you are learning Portuguese and you are a native Spanish speaker, these two languages will have similarities. Or, if you're learning Chinese as a native Japanese speaker. Again, you may find it easier. However, if you are a native English speaker and you are learning Mandarin Chinese, this can be a bigger challenge. Don't shy away from it, though! Choosing a language that is closer in origin will ideally be easier to learn, but of course, everyone is different. Just know once you pick, you'll need to fully commit in order to make progress.

2. WHAT TYPE OF LEARNER ARE YOU?

Everyone learns differently and it's important to know what type of learner you are, especially to effectively learn another language. Forcing yourself to use methods that don't work for you will only cause frustration. The beautiful thing about learning languages is that there are so many ways to do it. If one method doesn't work for you, there are at least a dozen others. Discover whether listening, reading, writing, or "doing" is the most effective for you, then start with activities that include these concepts. So, if you are a reading/writing type of learner then begin by finding news articles, children's books, or even beginner novels and look through them to feel the overall structure and patterns of the language. If you are a kinesthetic learner (activity and movement), then try incorporating movement into the language. You can try dancing, acting, or games to begin with. These are just basic tips to get you started until you are advancing in your language ability.

3. START WITH THE BASICS

Most people feel panicked when learning a new language with absolutely no knowledge. Take it one step at a time, as it's easy to get overwhelmed thinking about all the verb tenses and vocabulary words. Start with simply listening to videos, music, or real-life conversations. You need to hear the language to get a good grasp on it before you can begin memorizing anything else. I just call this, "spending time" with the language. Spend time with it without necessarily interacting until you feel at ease with the sounds. Essentially, any type of listening activity will get you used to the rhythm of the language and will help you immensely. If you don't understand how the language flows, then you'll have trouble using it correctly. Begin to feel its familiarity. I recommend giving this a try before you make thousands of notecards, and eventually quit because it's too much.

4. NEXT STEP: NUMBERS, VOCABULARY, AND SIMPLE GRAMMAR STRUCTURE

After you've gotten the "feel" of a language, most people want to jump right into conjugating verbs and reading books. You think by skipping things like the alphabet, numbers, and basic grammar structure you will make it to fluency faster. You also assume that this basic knowledge will fall into place and you'll "just know them" later. Then some months later, you're standing in a coffee shop in Germany, when the barista rattles off your bill and you can't recall any numbers. This is when you think, "Oops, I should have spent more time on this." Numbers are so important, even though they feel low on the list of interests. This goes for basic grammar and vocabulary words like foods, colors, the weather etc. Study them early, and study them often. Trust me…they appear more often than it seems.

5. THE TOP 20/50/100/200 RULE.

The top 20/50/100/200 rule states that if you memorize the top 20/50/100/200 most used words in a language, you'll be able to understand more of the language right away. Think about your native language, you tend to use the same words and verbs over and over. You use words such as, "I, house, dog, eat, sleep, work, fruit, cold, sweater," etc. If you know these words, your language ability will appear higher than it is, because of the high usage in the language every day. If you only know the top 20 most used words, you're better off than knowing none of them! And if you know the top 200 most used words in your target language, then you're well on your way to being able to converse, read, and write better. This is an easy goal. You can search online, "The top 100 most used words in Brazilian Portuguese". You'll find a list, so start learning those. Those lists will give you a wonderful starting point.

6.STUDY VOCABULARY AND VERBS RELATED TO THE THINGS YOU ENJOY TALKING ABOUT

When you first start talking with others in your target language, they're going to ask you about yourself. What are your hobbies? Where are you from? What is your job? These kinds of questions are going to come up often and a good rule is to learn vocabulary relating to these subjects. So, if you are a nurse and you enjoy traveling then you'll want to brush up on words related to nursing and travel. You may want to know how to describe what your job entails, when you work, adjectives about working conditions, and what your next adventure is. Relating to your life, you'll need to know how to say things like, "I like to do ____", "I want to do _____" and "I have done ____" for starters. These will be important beginning sentences to use while discussing yourself. This isn't only about you as well, though. The more varied subjects you can talk about, the more you can understand other people. You might have interests in common with someone you've just met on the road.

7. LEARN TO RECOGNIZE PAST TENSE AND FUTURE TENSE WHILE LEARNING THE PRESENT TENSE

Many resources will tell you to begin learning the present verb tenses before any others. Generally, this is a good rule, but it can also hold you back. My advice is to study the present tense, but also familiarize yourself with the past tense and the future tense. If you only focus on one tense, you can end up not being able to use the others well later, because you are in the habit of only producing one type. Trust me, when learning a new language, being able to recognize all three is very important from the start. However, there is more than one type of past, future, and present tenses. There is no need to overwhelm yourself with all of them, just recognize the most common ones. The tenses you need to focus on vary by language, so look at your target language and what tenses exist. Some languages don't use verb tenses like others, they are all unique. This is mostly advice for those learning Latin-based languages such as Spanish, French, German, Polish, etc. Recognizing various verb tenses early on will save you stress later!

8. FOCUS ON A PLACE OR ACCENT

The beauty and struggle of learning another language is focusing on what "culture/accent" of that language you want to learn. Example: Mexican Spanish vs. Colombian Spanish vs. Spain Spanish. Believe it or not, they are different. If a non-native English speaker is learning English, they focus on either American English, British English, or Australian English. That student cannot simply study *English* without a focus area, or their vocabulary can be scattered, as well as their accent. Hint: think about British slang and spelling. The word color in Britain is spelled "colour", and in the USA it's "color". However, focusing on one area doesn't mean you must ignore the other dialects, it just means that you need to know language varies depending on location. Decide where you live and why you are studying this language. Then base your intended focus on your target population that you will be interacting with the most. Back to the Spanish example, if you are learning Spanish and you live in the USA- you may want to study Mexican Spanish. However, if you live in France, then you are much more likely to interact with Spanish people (from Spain) so you may want to study Spain Spanish. You'll still be able to interact with anyone who speaks the Spanish language, but your vocabulary will vary.

9. READING, WRITING, SPEAKING AND LISTENING

Reading, writing, speaking, and listening are different skills. You'll need to practice each of them individually. Most of us don't realize they are separate skills! There are many people who spend all their time on one skill and ignore the others. Then as time goes by, they can speak well with others but can hardly read a book. Or, they spend all their time reading and cannot speak correctly. Start by working on each of these skills but put an emphasis on the ones that are the most important for your goals. Personally, I spend a lot of time on listening and speaking vs. writing or reading. So, my foreign language writing skills are worse than my listening skills! This is because I use language to travel and have conversations, so writing isn't as necessary. If you are learning French in order to do businesses with French companies, you may want to focus on reading and writing to converse via emails and letters. Your approach is unique to your desired goal!

10. LEARN LIKE A CHILD

This sounds silly, but it's true. When you begin using new words and phrases, you'll feel like a child who can hardly express what they want! In a sense you are. You may only have the vocabulary of a three-year-old in Italian, Japanese, or whatever language you are learning. You may feel frustrated because you want to say so much, but you have a limited vocabulary. That's ok, keep working. All children eventually learn new vocabulary words and phrases by exposure. Even with your minimal language ability, don't shy away from using it. Over time you'll become exposed to more words and your knowledge will grow. So, act like a child for now. Use simple phrases, mime what you need, and ask a "parent" (experienced speaker) how to say something or what a word means. If you know enough supporting words for what you are trying to say, then you'll need to improvise. The other speaker can understand your overall meaning and guide you. So, you want to say, "When I eat apples, I get a stomach ache." But you only know the words, "eat, apple, stomach, bad". Then use these words. Put together a badly worded sentence like, "When I eat apples, stomach is bad". The speaker will correct you. Repeat it. Write it down. Remember it.

11. TRY AND USE THIS NEW LANGUAGE IN ALL PARTS OF YOUR LIFE

Take notes, talk to yourself, talk to your dog, mock-reply to a work email, etc. in order to use the language in many ways. Contextual learning is so important if you want to master anything. Contextual learning means you are using that skill in context, or a real-life scenario. Look at all the little things you do in your native language daily. Maybe you like to talk to your houseplants or you make a grocery list. The more "little things" you do in your target language, the broader your knowledge will become. If you've got a "to-do" list, try writing it in Russian or Arabic for example. If you write in a journal, do this in your new language too. You'll learn more vocabulary in context and have a better time recalling it later.

12. SET CLEAR GOALS

Make clear goals about where you want to be and when. You can choose goals based on time or activity. An example could be, "I'd like to read and understand a novel by the end of the year." Or, "I want to know the top 500 words in 2 months." This will give you short term goals that contribute to longer term progress. If your long-term goal is to speak fluently, then these small goals will help you achieve that. Your goals depend on what you want to do with the language. If you are learning a language for work, then your goal may look like this, "I want to write 5 mock business emails in Japanese by the end of the winter." Any goal is better than no goal.

13. MAKE A SCHEDULE

This rule is important, even though I never seem to stick to mine. For those who thrive with plans and lists, this one can really help you. Like anything else in life, it's essential to stay on track. Oftentimes, you'll wake up and say that you'll study for an hour but then time gets away from you. Without a clear schedule, you won't reach any of your language goals. Take a moment when you begin learning a language to have a plan in place. You can always adjust it later if it doesn't suit you. Make a calendar and stick to it. Once it's a habit, it'll be harder to break!

14. THE MORE RESOURCES, THE MERRIER

One resource isn't enough to learn a language. It would be great if you could just attend one class or watch videos online and become fluent in a few months. But, that's rarely the case. It's important to use a variety of resources. Many language learners use various options such as online videos, books, phone apps, in-person classes, blogs, both online and face-to-face tutors, and conversational groups. I've personally tried all these options with one language or another, and they all offer different benefits. If you prefer in-person learning, you can always find classes and then use other resources as a secondary practice method. Or, you may prefer studying alone via online videos and blogs. Try a mix of all the resources available to you and some approaches will feel better than others.

15. USE MUSIC

Don't underestimate the power of music! Finding music that you enjoy in your target language is the easiest way to learn new vocabulary. Listening to music is also a great way to hear how native speakers formulate sentences, use slang, and hear the most common words. I've learned so many new words and phrases with music alone, and it's been my top tool when I learned Spanish. There are lists made for each country on Spotify, so you can search and find an entire list of music available in whatever language you choose. This will also help you understand some of the culture behind the language, too. In addition, you can search online for the "top hits today" if you prefer that route. EX: Google "Top Songs in Swedish 2018". Just dive in and it'll lead you to a world of options.

16. WITH LANGUAGE COMES CULTURE

Language and culture are deeply intertwined. You'll need to spend some time learning about the culture/s behind the language you're learning if you want to succeed. Culture influences language in a huge way, and often you'll hear cultural references in everyday conversations, so it's essential to educate yourself. If you are interested in learning about family dynamics, food, fashion, history, or something else, then learn about these aspects. You don't need to become an expert on the subject but try and learn a little bit about the culture. Language is all about communicating with people, and most likely since you're learning a foreign language, you will be communicating with people from another culture. If you want to learn from those people, you'll have to understand some of their roots. A simple online search will give a good start.

17. AT TIMES, YOU'LL FEEL UNCOMFORTABLE

Remember: learning a language is a skill. Like any skill you're going to make mistakes in order to grow. You're learning a new way to speak that can be very different from what you're used to. This often requires trial and error. Don't take it personally if a native speaker (or experienced speaker) corrects something you said. Instead, take it as a compliment. They want to help you succeed. Almost every language learner gets nervous about speaking in their target language, so they avoid doing it at all costs. They sit in their rooms practicing alone, never willing to use the language in real life. We've all been there, and you'll likely find yourself feeling this at some point in your language learning journey. Interacting in a new language is scary at first but find the courage to do it because it's the only way to help you really improve. Typically, native speakers get excited meeting someone who is interested in their language and culture! They'll ask you a ton of questions about why you want to learn that language. This experience is a perfect way to meet new friends from around the world, or even in your neighborhood.

18. SOME DAYS YOU'LL UNDERSTAND EVERYTHING, OTHER DAYS YOU'LL UNDERSTAND NOTHING

Even this still baffles me. There are days where you watch a TV show or listen to a Podcast in your target language and you understand almost everything. Yes, finally! You're on top of the world and all your hard work is paying off! Then the next day you meet someone at the supermarket and you can't understand more than two words they say. Those are the days you feel terrible, like you've learned nothing at all. Why spend hours and hours only to get nowhere? We all have those days of joy and those days of lows. Take it in stride, you're learning a lot and that's what matters. Everyone speaks differently and sometimes you may understand more in one situation than another. It could be due to accents used, the topic discussed, or just your state of mind that day. Pick yourself back up and keep going.

19. GETTING CORRECTED IS KEY

This is like what was mentioned before, but it requires some explanation. If you haven't been corrected by an experienced speaker, then wait for your time. Learning a foreign language will be filled with times when you'll make mistakes. Sometimes big mistakes. And in all honesty, you'll probably be making millions of them. What's important is not being afraid to do so. There is nothing to be ashamed about, but I know it can feel awkward and maddening. You've worked so hard and you thought you were speaking well, but usually that's not the case at the beginning. You may be talking with someone and they'll stop you and correct what you just said. This can throw you off, and you might feel embarrassed to talk again. But understand that mistakes are proof you are growing and learning. Don't let an experienced speaker make you feel bad about your ability! After you get corrected, it will stick with you. Take this as a learning opportunity, and you now know more than you did before. Next time, you won't make the same mistake. This is all part of the process.

20. TALK TO YOURSELF, A LOT

We all talk to ourselves, whether it's having a conversation, debate, or just little personal side-comments. Embrace talking to yourself in another language just like you do in English. When you are showering in the morning, practice having a conversation about the weather or pretend you are on a date with someone discussing your hobbies. The more you create "pretend conversations" and scenarios, the better prepared you are for when they appear in real life. Trust me, act out how to introduce yourself and how to ask personal questions. This is great for speaking practice and since you already do it in your native language, then do it in your other languages as well! When I started learning French, I would have dinner conversations with myself. I'd explain where I lived, what my hobbies were, and my opinions on certain social topics. You can play both roles. You may think this sounds silly, but it's quite fun once you get used to it.

21. NATIVE SPEAKERS CAN BE YOUR BEST TOOL

When you begin learning a language, the image that likely comes to mind is being on a level of fluency close to a native speaker. This is a hard level to reach unless you are immersed in the language for some time. If you really want to be fluent you may have to live where the language is the dominant one for a while. For now, native speakers can be a great resource if you need practice with accents, or any questions. Keep in mind that many times they don't understand why something is said the way it is, they just know it "sounds right." If learning specific rules behind grammar is essential for you, then natives may not be able to help define those. But they can absolutely guide you to sound more natural. Think about how you speak in your native language, if someone asked you why a certain sentence is placed in that order or a word is used in a certain context and not another, you may not know the exact rules behind it. You only know it "feels right" to say it that way. Find native speakers in your area if you can.

22. IMITATE NATIVE SPEAKERS, TOO

Just like stated above, native speakers are a great resource to use. But there is more to utilizing native speakers than simply listening passively to them. Watch the way that they form sounds and put together sentences. Focus on how their mouth moves, their facial expressions, and simple filler words. Filler words are words or phrases used in conversation to convey that someone is listening, thinking, or filling space that doesn't necessarily add to what's being said. In English, common filler words are: "like", "uhm", "I mean", "you know", "actually", "basically", and so on. After observing a native speaker, then put what you learned into action. Imitate native speakers accents as best you can, emphasize the same words in speech, mimic their facial expressions, and place your words in a similar order. All these things will help you to sound more natural.

23. TRAVEL IS THE BEST TEACHER

The beauty of learning languages is the ability to use them around the world. Depending on what language you are studying, it opens so much opportunity to travel. For example, if you are studying French you can visit France, Canada, or parts of Africa. There are so many amazing places around the world where you can use your new-found skill with locals. Take advantage of this and buy some plane tickets. Plus, who doesn't want an excuse for a vacation? In addition to traveling just for fun, going to a place where your target language is the official language is the best way to learn. Remember: contextual learning. You must order food, read street signs, ask for directions, and interact with locals. You will learn so much more than if you were at home. It's a wonderful learning opportunity to really grow your practical usage of the language.

24. LANGUAGE LEARNING APPS: FIND THE BEST ONE (OR FIVE) FOR YOU!

Most people have smartphones now, so remember that they are also a great tool for language learning. There are apps designed for thousands of languages to help learners just like you. Try doing a quick online search of the various phone apps for a specific language, there are dozens of options. I've tried many of them and some work better for certain languages than others. Many language learners online will provide you with an entire list of apps specific to that language you want to learn. Try a few options and see which works best for you! The wonderful thing is there are so many choices.

25. CONSISTENCY IS CRUCIAL

There is more progress with consistency than hours spent. Studying for 15 minutes a day will be more beneficial than studying for 3 hours once a week. Try and make time for language practice daily. Life is busy, and you probably have many things to do. But you won't get anywhere with your language if you don't invest consistent time. This can be simple, it doesn't need to take hours a day either. Try listening to a Podcast on the way to work in the morning or watching a movie while at the gym. You can also listen to music or spend 20 minutes on an app before bed. Once you incorporate it into your daily routine it will be easy to keep up with.

26. MOTIVATION WILL MAKE OR BREAK YOUR LEARNING

Remember back in high school and you had to go to a class that you had no interest in? Well, that's what learning a language is like if you are not motivated. Therefore, picking a language you like is essential. However, if you are required to learn a language for another reason, you'll need to find a way to stay motivated. Whether that's because you can travel with work once you learn the language, or you can put it on your resume. Maybe your motivation is that you'll be able to speak to your spouse's parents or a new coworker. Your motivational tactics will depend on why you started learning that language to begin with. If you lose motivation to keep learning, you will end up stopping all together. Remind yourself why you started and give yourself rewards if necessary.

27. YOU MAY ALWAYS RETAIN SOME OF YOUR NATIVE ACCENT

In the language community, you'll find people discussing accents in relation to fluency. An idea exists that if you have an accent while speaking a different language, it means you aren't good at that language. This isn't true at all and don't believe that opinion if you hear it. For someone to have zero accent in another language is difficult, but not impossible. Try your best to sound as native as possible, because having a very thick accent can make it harder for people to understand you. However, some people are never able to get rid of some of their native accent and this is perfectly fine! There is nothing wrong with having an accent. An accent won't make you any better or worse of a language learner and speaker. Many people will find your accent endearing and it can spark conversations about where you're from, why you learned that language, and who you are.

28. KNOW SLANG

Slang, it's important. Take a day and listen to how others speak in your native language. Odds are, every speaker uses slang words and you do too. If you want to be able to speak to others in casual situations in your target language, you may want to focus on learning slang words and phrases. They will come up on TV, in music, and daily conversations a lot. Once you learn them, the more you'll see them! Also, you'll sound more fluent if you can use them correctly. Native speakers will be impressed, and it'll show how much you really know. You may choose not to use slang in your speech, but it is good to know it anyway.

29. KNOWING EVERY WORD VS. KNOWING THE GENERAL MEANING. WHAT TO FOCUS ON?

When you reach an intermediate level in your new language, you may begin to pick up on understanding "generalities". This means that when someone is speaking, you may not understand every word they use, but you understand the conversational topic and most of the key points stated. You understand generally what's being discussed, even though you may not catch every single word. This is what understanding the "general meaning" implies. Many learners focus on knowing every word, especially when reading or listening in their target language. Oftentimes, you'll only catch 70% or even less of the words. This is ok. If you understand the general idea of the conversation, then you are moving along just fine. You don't need to know absolutely everything in order to converse. Remember how many ways there are to say the same thing. If this happens to you, don't be discouraged.

30. IF YOU SPEAK ENGLISH, MOST PEOPLE WILL PREFER TO SPEAK ENGLISH WITH YOU

In every language learner's journey there comes a time when you are confident enough to travel and speak your target language with natives. This is also the time when you realize most people around the world will speak English instead. Often, the travelers you meet on the road will be speaking English with each other, even if it's not their native language. This is especially true if you stay in hostels. You may find someone from Germany, France, or Italy and they all seem to speak English with one another because it's the only language they have in common. This can be frustrating because you want to practice your language learning in real life, but you keep finding others that only speak English. Keep trying to find native speakers anyway. If someone does speak the language you want to learn, tell them you want to speak in their language instead. Likely, they'll be happy to converse with you.

31. WORK ON IMPROVING YOUR MEMORY

Your memory is key when language learning! How will you remember new words if your memory is lacking? Try fun games on your phone or get a tiny Sudoku book. Memory practice doesn't need to be anything serious, but the better your memory is, the better your language learning will be. Anything you do that causes you to learn, think, and plan can help you with memory. Learning a language is an exercise for memory, too.

32. THE "RECOGNITION RULE"

The more you come across a word, the more you'll recognize it. Seems obvious, right? Luckily, it is. There are going to be words that seem to appear at random in conversation, TV, and music. They seem familiar, but it isn't a word you hear every day, so you haven't bothered to memorize it. Or, you've tried to memorize it but can never seem to remember its definition. This can happen a lot. At some point even if you cannot recall the exact translation of the word, you'll understand the meaning. Eventually, this will happen because you've heard it used in context so many times, it got placed in your brain. Sometimes words can be learned by passively coming across them enough times. This isn't going to happen for an entire language, though, so don't throw away those notecards.

33. IF YOU CAN'T REMEMBER A WORD THEN WRITE IT SOMEWHERE YOU SEE IT EVERY DAY

The title says it all. Like mentioned above, there are some words that DO NOT stick in your head! I can name at least a dozen words in Spanish that I see all the time and can never remember. Sometimes it's frustrating. The easiest thing you can do is write down the word and place it somewhere you see it every day, many times a day if possible. A great spot is on your bathroom mirror or refrigerator. You access these places at least once a day and when you do, you'll be reminded of that word. Then write the definition with it. Someday you'll remember it.

34. EACH LANGUAGE IS UNIQUE

Don't get in the habit of comparing your native language to your target language, because this is unfair. Each language is its own entity and comparing them can cause you to become judgmental of the language or culture behind. Of course, you may prefer one over the other but they both offer different experiences. You can translate concepts for meaning, but no two languages are the same. Always comparing another language to, for example English, will ruin your acceptance and understanding of the language. Try to look at the foreign language as its own entity and not what it is in comparison to your native language. Accept a new language without judgement or superiority. Remember languages are indicators of cultures, each is interesting and beautiful.

35. TRANSLATION IS MORE THAN JUST WORD-TO-WORD EXCHANGES

This is especially important to know if you are interested in doing translation work. Languages are more than words strung together. There are so many pieces behind a language and if you want to know a language well enough to translate, then you must study more than just vocabulary words and common verbs. You'll need at least a minimum knowledge of culture, slang, colloquialisms, idioms, and more. Colloquialisms and idioms are ways of speaking in a language such as informal speaking methods, common expressions, or speech with figurative meaning. An idiom would be, "The grass is always greener on the other side." And a colloquialism example are the words, "gonna" and "ain't". So, you've got to know more than formal speaking to be a translator. Taking a translation course or simply doing an online search can highlight how detailed translation work can be. If you are ever in a situation where you need to translate between two people, even casually, you'll get a better understanding of how complicated this can be.

36. TRY A TARGET LANGUAGE CHALLENGE

Target Language Challenges are online challenges created by the language learning community. Monthly language challenges urge you to use language in fun, unique ways every day of the month. The challenges also change every month, so you can always find a new one when you finish. One day of the challenge could ask you to write a letter to a family member asking them how they are doing or make a list of all your dreams. The next day on the calendar may ask you to have a mock conversation with yourself about your daily routine. Challenges can be a fun way to interact with your target language for just a few minutes a day!

37. YOU MAY NEVER REACH FULL FLUENCY (C2)

Mentioned before, when you start learning a language you dream of reaching a high level of fluency, but sometimes that isn't attainable if you are not fully immersed. On the language learning scale, it begins with A1 and continues to C2. The scale is: A1 (total beginner), A2 (elementary beginner), B1 (early intermediate), B2 (upper intermediate), C1 (proficient or advanced), and finally C2 (fluent or near fluent). In your native language you are a C2, as an adult. Reaching this level of fluency is difficult and often includes full immersion or daily contextual use. If you use that language for work or family matters, you probably use it very often. Therefore, your ability to reach fluency is greater than if you only use it when you travel. Again, your goals will determine how skilled you want to become. If speaking without much difficulty is a good level for you, then you may not want to reach full fluency. Remaining at a B1/2 level can be perfectly fine for you.

38. YOU'LL START SEEING AND HEARING THAT LANGUAGE EVERYWHERE

This can happen with anything in your life. The more you think about something, the more it seems to appear around you. You just started studying Swedish and have never noticed it in your city before. Now all the sudden, you overhear a woman on her cell phone speaking Swedish. You see Swedish written on labels at the grocery store. You're reading a book in English and they use a random Swedish word. You wonder, "Was Swedish everywhere before and I just never noticed it?" Probably. This experience will happen with any language you practice and learn. Languages are everywhere and once you open your eyes, you'll see them.

39. LEARNING A NEW LANGUAGE CAN HELP YOU LEARN MORE ABOUT YOUR OWN LANGUAGE

Are you learning a Romance language such as Spanish, Italian, Portuguese, or French? If so, you'll find they are closely related with English in many ways. You'll see similar words and phrases. Occasionally you'll learn a word in your target language that looks like a word you already recognize from your native language. Then, when you look up the meaning of the word, you find it is almost identical to the word in English! This makes it easier to remember, and now you are reminded of a word in your native language too. This situation happened to me just a few hours ago. The word, "Tumultuosa" appeared in a Spanish video and I was reminded of

41

the English word "Tumultuous." It's a word I hardly use, but now I won't forget the meaning in Spanish because it's almost identical to a word I already know. If you are someone who isn't a fan of grammar, learning a second language can change your understanding of how grammar works in your native language.

40. LEARNING A NEW LANGUAGE CAN SOMETIMES HINDER YOUR NATIVE LANGUAGE ABILITY

Sometimes words or concepts just make more sense in another language. Often when you are close with a language, you'll want to use it in situations that feel natural. Again, languages are unique, and sometimes it makes more sense to use another language rather than your native one. You'll incorporate new words, phrases, or ideas into your own English vocabulary over your language learning journey. Out of nowhere you'll use, *"C'est ridicule!"* (that's ridiculous) when talking to yourself at work. Another situation you'll experience is when you remember a word in your second (or third, fourth, etc.) language and not in your native language. You will be talking to someone and can't find the word for "motorbike" in English but will remember it in French instead. There are words you will begin to forget in one language and pick up in another. Have you heard a bilingual speaker switch between languages when they speak? This can become you and it's fun!

41. LANGUAGE LEARNING IS GREAT FOR YOUR BRAIN

A better memory and increased focus are just some of the positives changes that languages make to your brain. Remember that the brain is a muscle, it needs to be exercised. Learning a language exercises and strengthens your brain. Each brain is unique and the benefits you'll get from learning a language is exclusive to you. There have been numerous studies about how learning a language truly increases brain function and keeps it healthier longer. Being bilingual is great for more than just travel and enjoyment!

42. LANGUAGE PLATEAU HAPPENS, DISCOVER HOW TO KEEP IMPROVING

All language learners loathe the plateau stage. The plateau stage is when you are stuck in your learning and you can't seem to advance to the next level. EX: from B2 to C1, the language levels we discussed earlier. This usually happens in the intermediate levels when you are trying to reach the advanced stages of a language. The plateau period can be tough to break away from. My advice is to jump into immersion situations. Watch a lot of TV shows, read many books, and speak often. Really often. You'll find new words that you need in specific situations that you didn't realize that you needed. Write down these words/verbs and study them. Your vocabulary will grow immensely.

43. THERE'S ALWAYS MORE TO LEARN

You'll never finish learning a language. You'll never know every single word even in your own native language. Also, languages are always evolving, it makes them feel alive in a sense. Look at history, even recent history. Slang words appear every few years and the words your parents used when they were young are probably different from what you use. Shakespearean English is also a great example to see how much has changed in only a few hundred years. This is the same with any language, too. When you take on the challenge of learning a language, always remember that you'll be learning for life! It's fun and it keeps things exciting.

44. BURN-OUT

At some point, the "burn out" phrase will come. At first, you may invest a lot of time into learning your target language and after a while, your energy is drained. At the beginning, it can take some time to get a routine and immediately you see a huge improvement in your ability. Then months later, you'll get tired and possibly bored. There is no harm in taking a few days, or even a week off. There are times I've taken months off. Relaxing can help all that information settle into your brain. Everyone needs a break occasionally. Again, your brain is a muscle and it's been working hard. Give it some rest.

45. YOU MAY HAVE DIFFERENT PERSONALITIES IN DIFFERENT LANGUAGES

If you are someone who already speaks another language, then you've probably experienced firsthand. Languages have personalities and they are directly influenced by the cultures in which they originate. When you use different languages, it can change the way you speak and act. Of course, this does not mean you are a completely different person. But rather, you pick up on the culture of the language and tend to speak like natives. For instance, if you speak German and Italian, you may express yourself differently when using each one. In German, you could be more direct and formal and in Italian you tend to talk by using more colorful and dramatic expressions. Even if you are saying the same thing, the language you use can influence how you speak. Sometimes people feel more brave, loud, or thoughtful in one language or another. When you reach a good level in your target language and you are speaking with flow, notice the difference between that language and your native language. Is there any difference for you?

46. YOU CAN DREAM IN A DIFFERENT LANGUAGE

This is a fun part people don't expect. If you are spending many hours learning, speaking, and practicing a new language, it can carry over to your dream state. I've experienced dreaming in various languages including French, Spanish, and Italian. If you dream in another language and remember your dreams after waking up, you may be really impressed with yourself. You accessed all that subconscious knowledge! In addition to dreaming, you may start thinking in that language too. It's often debated whether we think in languages or in concepts, but sometimes you may think about something in whatever language you've been using most. Either way, enjoy the feeling of progress!

47. LANGUAGE LOSS. USE IT OR LOSE IT

The title says it all. Languages need to be used to be retained. If you were expecting to learn a language, then not use it for a year and have it stay perfectly intact, then I'm sorry to let you down. Language loss is very real, and you'll need to keep talking, reading, writing, and listening to maintaining your level. Luckily, once you've reached a good momentum in your new language then you can watch movies, read a book, or speak with others to keep it fresh. You don't necessarily need to keep memorizing new words. Just remember to use it every so often!

48. YOU'LL WANT TO LEARN MORE LANGUAGES

Languages are so much more than words. After learning one language well (or even just after you start to learn one), you'll get addicted to how different the world seems now. New languages can make you feel as though your eyes have been opened for the first time. Especially if you only knew one language, then learning a second can completely change your life perspective. You'll begin to see how many ways there are to exist and express yourself. Most language learners get obsessed with language learning and try to learn as many languages as possible. No matter why you began learning to begin with, you will become so interested in everything the world has to offer.

49. ONCE YOU LEARN ONE LANGUAGE, THEN LEARNING ANOTHER ONE BECOMES EASIER

This is especially true if the languages are in the same family. If you learned French and now you want to learn Spanish, it's going to be much easier. So many words and grammar concepts overlap so you don't have to relearn key aspects, you just apply new words. Even if the languages aren't related, you now understand methods and approaches of language learning and how to practice them efficiently. You learned more than just a language, you learned a new skill too.

50. YOU SHOULD ENJOY YOURSELF

At the end of the day, learning a new language should be fun. Take some pressure off yourself and enjoy the process. Although it can be frustrating at times, you'll be so excited to grow and use this new language in your everyday life. Take your time and trust yourself!

OTHER HELPFUL RESOURCES:

Youtube, SpanishPod101 (PortuguesPod101, KoreanPod101) etc.

Many of the most popular languages will have a Youtube channel called _____Pod101.

Phone apps that are often used for language learning are: Duolingo, LingoDeer, Memrise, Babbel, HelloChinese, HelloTalk, Busuu, and iTalki.

You can also find tons of books at any local bookstore or online through Amazon.

Lastly, you can search online to find language speaking groups or formal classes.

Apps/online dictionaries to download: Reverso, SpanishDict

Youtube.com (very specific to languages)
Duolingo: https://www.duolingo.com/
Dictionaries: reverso.com, spanishdict.com, bonpatron.com (French), Google Translate

READ OTHER

50 THINGS TO KNOW

BOOKS

50 Things to Know

Website: 50thingstoknow.com

Facebook: facebook.com/50thingstoknow

Pinterest: pinterest.com/lbrennec

YouTube: youtube.com/user/50ThingsToKnow

Twitter: twitter.com/50ttk

Mailing List: Join the 50 Things to Know
Mailing List to Learn About New Releases

50 Things to Know

Please leave your honest review of this book on Amazon and Goodreads. We appreciate your positive and constructive feedback. Thank you.

Made in the USA
Monee, IL
15 July 2024

61832423R00042